cross stitch

Home
Sweet Home

MODERN CROSS STITCH DESIGNS
FOR HOME AND GARDEN

CHERYL MCKINNON
of Tiny Modernist

Tuva Publishing
www.tuvapublishing.com

Address Merkez Mah. Cavusbasi Cad. No71
Cekmekoy - Istanbul 34782 / Turkey
Tel +9 0216 642 62 62

Home Sweet Home

First Print January / 2023

All Global Copyrights Belong To
Tuva Tekstil ve Yayıncılık Ltd.

Content Cross Stitch

Editor in Chief Ayhan DEMİRPEHLİVAN
Project Editor Kader DEMİRPEHLİVAN
Author Cheryl McKinnon
Technical Editor Leyla ARAS
Graphic Designers Ömer ALP, Abdullah BAYRAKÇI,
Tarık TOKGÖZ
Photograph Tuva Publishing

ISBN 978-605-7834-66-9

 TuvaYayincilik   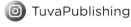 TuvaPublishing

 TuvaYayincilik    TuvaPublishing

Contents

Introduction 11
Charts 58
The Stitches 94

Projects

Project Gallery

Page 14

Page 16

Page 18

Page 20

Page 22

Page 24

Page 26

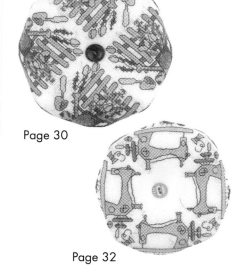

Page 30

Page 32

Page 34

Page 36

Page 38

Page 40

Page 42

Page 44

Page 48

Page 50

Page 46

Page 52

Page 54

Page 56

introduction

Cross stitch is one of the easiest forms of needlework to learn - and it's so enjoyable. Stitching can be used as form of mind relaxing, it helps to de-stress, and the best part is that you are creating beautiful keepsake heirlooms.

It's also a very beautiful form of self-expression, where you get to decide how to create the artwork. You can choose to follow the chart, or customize your threads and fabrics to fit your own style.

This book is meant to celebrate hobbies, arts, crafts, and everything wonderful about home life - from flowers and gardening to sewing, seasonal houses, and kitchen motifs.

I hope this book will inspire you with the many fun, bright designs to choose from - so I encourage you to take some time for yourself, sit and relax with a mug of your favourite warm beverage, and enjoy stitching something for your Home Sweet Home.

Cheryl McKinnon

Among the Wildflowers

This quote is a favourite, and makes me think of lovely summer
days, walking through fields of flowers with no cares in the world.
Wouldn't it be a lovely way to spend the afternoon?
Stitch this design to bring some of that feeling into your life!

materials needed

Fabric: DMC 14ct Aida (DM222/712)

Colour: Off - White

Fabric Size: 40 x 35cm

Stitch Count: 121w x 97h

Design Size: 22 x 18cm

Needle: DMC Cross-Stitch No:26
(Art:1771/3)

Thread: DMC Mouline Stranded Cotton

DMC Floss: 3865, 745, 743, 742, 353, 352, 3609,
3607, 157, 794, 164, 989, 987, 414, 434 and 413

Cross Stitch: 2 strands / **Back Stitch:** 1 strand

Chart on Page 60 - 61

Baking Sampler

Show your family and guests that your baking is "made with love", with this sampler featuring vintage-inspired kitchen items, delicious ingredients and a white lace border to tie it all together. A home wouldn't be complete without the smell of baking, licking the spoon and eating the treats once they're done!

materials needed

Fabric: Zweigart 27ct Evenweave Linda (1235/3009)
Colour: Misty Rose
Fabric Size: 40 x 40cm
Stitch Count: 131w x 131h
Design Size: 24 x 24cm

Needle: DMC Cross-Stitch No:26 (Art:1771/3)
Thread: DMC Mouline Stranded Cotton
DMC Floss: B5200, 744, 743, 353, 352, 350, 964, 959, 3812, 907, 437, 435, 168, 169 and 413
Cross Stitch: 2 strands / **Back Stitch:** 1 strand
Chart on Page 62 - 63

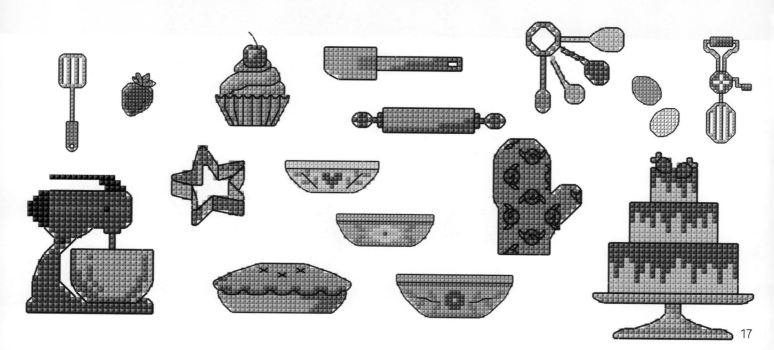

Coffee Banner

Do you love coffee? This piece features a coffee grinder,
a delicious-looking latte and cappuccino, and tasty pastries!
Frame and display it in your kitchen, workplace, or anywhere you
sip your favourite hot beverage. It can also be finished as a Bell
Pull, adding a fabric backing and making a rod pocket at the top
for a hanger.

materials needed

Fabric: 28ct DMC Linen (DM432SO/B5200)
Colour: White
Fabric Size: 28 x 50cm
Stitch Count: 70w x 198h
Design Size: 12 x 36cm

Needle: DMC Cross-Stitch No:26 (Art:1771/3)
Thread: DMC Mouline Stranded Cotton
DMC Floss: Ecru, 677, 353, 352, 3811, 3849, 3848, 3847, 906, 904, 437, 435, 433, 762, 168, 169 and 3799
Cross Stitch: 2 strands / **Back Stitch:** 1 strand

Chart on Page 64 - 65

tea time Banner

Are you a tea drinker? This lovely fresh design features so many delightful teas and desserts. So sit and have a cuppa while you stitch this one! Frame and display it in your kitchen, workplace, or anywhere you sip your favourite hot beverage. It can also be finished as a Bell Pull, adding a fabric backing and making a rod pocket at the top for a hanger.

materials needed

Fabric: DMC 28ct Linen (DM432SO/B5200)
Colour: White
Fabric Size: 28 x 50cm
Stitch Count: 70w x 198h
Design Size: 12 x 36cm

Needle: DMC Cross-Stitch No:26 (Art:1771/3)
Thread: DMC Mouline Stranded Cotton
DMC Floss: 712, 677, 745, 743, 436, 963, 3326, 899, 335, 309, 772, 907, 905, 168, 169 and 3799
Cross Stitch: 2 strands / **Back Stitch:** 1 strand

Chart on Page 66 - 67

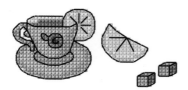

Craftiness is Happiness

Add a splash of colour and style to your craft room or children's room with this modern sampler-style design. The colours and motifs are bright and fun to match any space. Or try stitching a few of the motifs separately as a greeting card or gift tag for your crafty friends!

materials needed

Fabric: DMC 14ct Aida (DM222/Blanc)
Colour: White
Fabric Size: 35 x 35cm
Stitch Count: 106w x 106h
Design Size: 20 x 20cm

Needle: DMC Cross-Stitch No:26 (Art:1771/3)
Thread: DMC Mouline Stranded Cotton
DMC Floss: Ecru, 3822, 3820, 722, 605, 604, 3608, 964, 958, 3761, 3760, 166, 988, 437, 435, 168, 169 and 535
Cross Stitch: 2 strands / **Back Stitch:** 1 strand

Chart on Page 68 - 69

23

y muy cerca de esta; una vez terminada esta anilla hacer pasar
el hilo con el cual se ha ven?do trabajando, por encima de la
mano izquierda, tomar la la...
mano derecha y ejecutar 6 d...
la labor = despues de lo...
vuelve a hacer una anilla...
cuidando de juntar las...
como se indi a en las fig...

Encaje de frivolité
Con una lanzadera hacer...
1 bag., 2 d. n., 1 bag...
2 d. n., 1 bag., 2 d. n...
larga, 1 d. n. = cerrar...
hilo — al revés — con...

Seguir como hemos...
formar el último d. n...
dente por medio de u...
baguilla larga, lue...
hacer el último d...
sujetar los hilos.

Cuando se ten...
terminadas las...
cientes anillas, lev...
las baguillas con...
de ganchillo dista...
unos de otros...
puntos de ca...
Encima de esta...
vuelta, repetir...
puesta de 1 p...
en el pilar d...
2 puntos de ca...
Para termin...
corto en la...
2ª bag.; 3 p...
cadeneta, 1...
vuelta de pi...

Encaje...
lanzaderas.
puede vers...
La 2ª y 3ª pasadas...
Enlázase el hilo de la lanzade...
1ª bag. donde se le sujeta; luego, con...

baguilla de la anilla

...cer con la lanzadera una
...suelta a la labor = despues
... milímetros de longitud,
= dejar de nuevo un hilo
suelto, empezar
...tercera anilla
...une des-
...del 4º d. n.
...5ª. bag. de
la primera anilla
...volver la labor
...pues de terminada anilla de
...a que todas
...las baguillas su-
...periores aparez-
...an al derecho y
...s baguillas infe-
...res al revés de
...or.

Cuando esta
tira deba servir
como entredó-
...ría, se
...ba-
...olié de
...illo por el
...de los que
...en en los
...s que si-

**Tira de frivo-
lité** (fig. 531).
...Anudar los dos cabos de hilo
...y con una lanzadera, hacer una
...según las fig. 529 y 530 = volver la labor =
...zadera hacer una anilla igual a la primera

...on dos
...según
...en la
...la mano

24

Spring Bird Bookmark

This cheery little bird is sitting on top of a lovely pot of violets.
Why not make this bookmark to remind yourself of spring all year round?

materials needed

Fabric: DMC 16ct Aida (DM842/Blanc)
Colour: White
Fabric Size: 15 x 25cm
Stitch Count: 38w x 94h
Design Size: 6 x 14cm

Needle: DMC Cross-Stitch No:26 (Art:1771/3)
Thread: DMC Mouline Stranded Cotton
DMC Floss: 712, 745, 211, 209, 3837, 3348, 3347, 3346, 437, 435, 434, 168, 169 and 413
Cross Stitch: 2 strands / **Back Stitch:** 1 strand

Chart on Page 82

Home
Sweet Home

The bright decorative lettering in this design is a fun take on a classic sampler. Paired with five modern houses of all shapes and sizes and bright florals peeking out around them, this design would look great in an entryway, mud room, or in your living room as a lovely welcome for guests.

materials needed

Fabric: DMC 16ct Aida (DM842/Blanc)
Colour: White
Fabric Size: 40 x 45cm
Stitch Count: 124w x 164h
Design Size: 20 x 26cm

Needle: DMC Cross-Stitch No:26 (Art:1771/3)
Thread: DMC Mouline Stranded Cotton
DMC Floss: 712, 3822, 3820, 605, 3341, 608, 826, 959, 954, 907, 905, 169 and 413
Cross Stitch: 2 strands / **Back Stitch:** 1 strand

Chart on Page 70 - 71

Gardening Biscornu

Biscornu are one of my favourite finishes - they are sweet little pillows that can be used as pin cushions, or stacked to become a decorative item for a curio shelf. These ones would make a great gift for anyone who gardening!

materials needed

Fabric: DMC 28ct Evenweave (DM542A/Blanc)
Colour: White
Fabric Size: 20 x 20cm
Stitch Count: 63w x 64h
Design Size: 12 x 12cm

Needle: DMC Cross-Stitch No:26 (Art:1771/3)
Thread: DMC Mouline Stranded Cotton
DMC Floss: 3822, 3609, 3607, 159, 160, 161, 989, 987, 437, 435 and 413
Cross Stitch: 2 strands / **Back Stitch:** 1 strand
Chart on Page 72

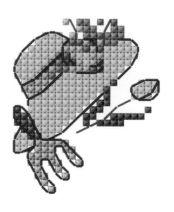

Sewing Biscornu

Such a sweet sewing design - with tiny buttons, pins, sewing machines and thread. Try using this biscornu as a pin cushion in the sewing room, or make it for a crafty friend as a gift!

materials needed

Fabric: DMC 28ct Evenweave (DM542A/Blanc)
Colour: White
Fabric Size: 20 x 20cm
Stitch Count: 62w x 62h
Design Size: 12 x 12cm

Needle: DMC Cross-Stitch No:26 (Art:1771/3)
Thread: DMC Mouline Stranded Cotton
DMC Floss: 3822, 604, 964, 958, 913, 415 and 413

Cross Stitch: 2 strands / **Back Stitch:** 1 strand / **French Knot:** 2 strands

Chart on Page 73

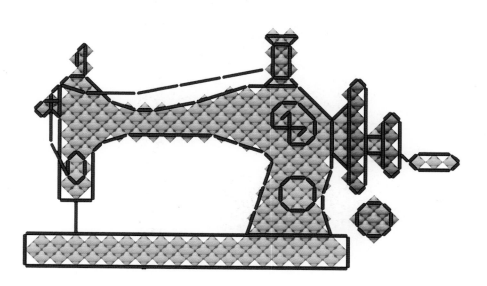

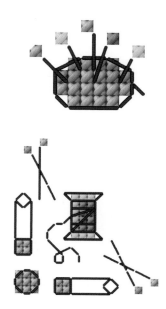

One Stitch at a time

Sewing designs are always a stylish addition to your home! These bold purple flowers and sewing motifs would look great in any sewing room or craft space! Don't have any purple in your home? Try switching up the colours to match your own decor.

materials needed

Fabric: DMC 28ct Evenweave (DM542A/Blanc)
Colour: White
Fabric Size: 35 x 45cm
Stitch Count: 96w x 148h
Design Size: 18 x 28cm

Needle: DMC Cross-Stitch No:26 (Art:1771/3)
Thread: DMC Mouline Stranded Cotton
DMC Floss: 211, 554, 553, 552, 550, 907, 906, 904, 3072, 648, 647, 646 and 3371
Cross Stitch: 2 strands / **Back Stitch:** 1 strand

Chart on Page 74 - 75

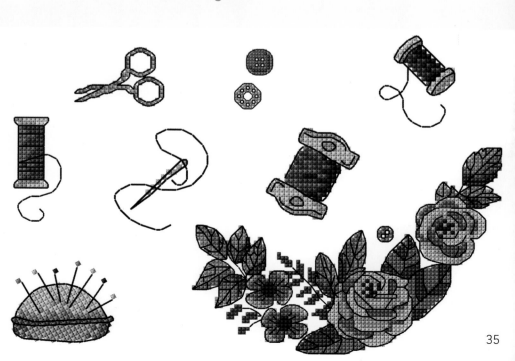

Spring Robin

Spring is such a beautiful season, when the air gets fresh & warm, and the outside world comes alive again after a cold winter. This designs remind me of spring - the smell of fresh dirt in the garden, picking strawberries, seeing tiny spring flowers come up, and watching robins hop on the lawn.

materials needed

Fabric: Zweigart 32ct Belfast (Petit Point/7349)
Colour: Gray
Fabric Size: 30 x 30cm
Stitch Count: 76w x 77h
Design Size: 12 x 12cm

Needle: DMC Cross-Stitch No:26 (Art:1771/3)
Thread: DMC Mouline Stranded Cotton
DMC Floss: Blanc, 3822, 3820, 722, 720, 351, 349, 3609, 3607, 26, 209, 3746, 907, 905, 762, 168, 437, 435, 640 and 3799
Cross Stitch: 2 strands / **Back Stitch:** 1 strand

Chart on Page 76

Vintage Beehive

Beautiful this vintage-inspired beehive, in faded golds, creams, pinks and mauves, with large flowers and delicate back stitch details. This gorgeous garden scene would make a lovely framed picture or be quite striking finished as the front of a throw cushion.

materials needed

Fabric: DMC 25ct Evenweave (DM532/772)
Colour: Light Green
Fabric Size: 40 x 40cm
Stitch Count: 97w x 96h
Design Size: 19 x 19cm

Needle: DMC Cross-Stitch No:26 (Art:1771/3)
Thread: DMC Mouline Stranded Cotton
DMC Floss: 712, 745, 743, 761, 3712, 3609, 3607, 210, 209, 912, 907, 906, 3348, 3347, 367, 677, 729, 3829 and 3790
Cross Stitch: 2 strands / **Back Stitch:** 1 strand

Chart on Page 77

Four Seasonal Houses

This pretty set features seasonal scenes with matching white borders. Try stitching them separately and switching them out in a frame for each season. Or stitched together as a sampler, they would make a beautiful year-round addition to your decor.

materials needed

Fabric: Zweigart 28ct Brittney Lugana (3270/779)
Colour: Dark Beige
Fabric Size: 45 x 45cm
Stitch Count: 144w x 144h
Design Size: 25 x 25cm

Needle: DMC Cross-Stitch No:26 (Art:1771/3)
Thread: DMC Mouline Stranded Cotton
DMC Floss: Blanc, 3822, 3820, 353, 352, 921, 3811, 3810, 166, 580, 642, 646 and 535
Cross Stitch: 2 strands / **Back Stitch:** 1 strand
Chart on Page 78 - 81

Little Cactus Blooms

Cactus designs bring a cheerful summer feeling into your home
any time of the year! This little piece will stitch up quickly, making
a nice gift when finished in a hoop or frame.

materials needed

Fabric: DMC 14ct Aida (DM222/Blanc)
Colour: White
Fabric Size: 25 x 25cm
Stitch Count: 49w x 48h
Design Size: 9 x 9cm

Needle: DMC Cross-Stitch No:26 (Art:1771/3)
Thread: DMC Mouline Stranded Cotton
DMC Floss: 3713, 3716, 3733, 564, 913, 562, 561, 168, 169 and 3799
Cross Stitch: 2 strands / **Back Stitch:** 1 strand

Chart on Page 83

Little House with Wreath

Tiny designs are perfect for a quick stitch, and this one would
work in a hoop, framed or stitched up as a greeting card.
The fresh, bright colours will complement any space in your house.

materials needed

Fabric: DMC 28ct Evenweave
Colour: Blue
Fabric Size: 25 x 25cm
Stitch Count: 57w x 57h
Design Size: 10 x 10cm

Needle: DMC Cross-Stitch No:26 (Art:1771/3)
Thread: DMC Mouline Stranded Cotton
DMC Floss: B5200, 3823, 3822, 3820, 3713,
604, 964, 3812, 704, 905 and 801
Cross Stitch: 2 strands / **Back Stitch:** 1 strand

Chart on Page 83

Nighttime Moths

Transport yourself into this gorgeous nighttime scene - with moths, mushrooms, beautiful night blooms, bright stars and the moon all stitched on a soothing dark background. Have a difficult time stitching on dark fabrics? Try placing a piece of white paper below your stitching to help see the holes.

materials needed

Fabric: DMC 14ct Aida (DM222/792)
Colour: Navy Blue
Fabric Size: 30 x 30cm
Stitch Count: 75w x 75h
Design Size: 14 x 14cm

Needle: DMC Cross-Stitch No:26 (Art:1771/3)
Thread: DMC Mouline Stranded Cotton
DMC Floss: B5200, 3823, 3822, 353, 352, 350, 747, 519, 211, 209, 955, 954, 3072, 648 and 646
Cross Stitch: 2 strands / **Back Stitch:** 1 strand

Chart on Page 84

Sewing Machine with Flowers

I love vintage sewing machines - they have so much charm and beautiful decorative elements. Paired with some bright flowers, this sewing machine design will add instant vintage-inspired chic anywhere in your house!

materials needed

Fabric: DMC 14ct Aida (DM222/Blanc)
Colour: White
Fabric Size: 35 x 30cm
Stitch Count: 96w x 71h
Design Size: 18 x 13cm

Needle: DMC Cross-Stitch No:26 (Art:1771/3)
Thread: DMC Mouline Stranded Cotton
DMC Floss: 712, 745, 743, 353, 352, 350, 164, 320, 907, 470, 842, 840, 169, 535 and 3799
Cross Stitch: 2 strands / **Back Stitch:** 1 strand

Chart on Page 85

Small Things with Great Love

This is a large statement piece that can adorn your house all year round. The saying is a beautiful reminder to be mindful and loving, and the decorative wording and large blooming flowers make this a design that is sure to lift your spirits.

materials needed

Fabric: DMC 28ct Evenweave (DM542A/Blanc)
Colour: White
Fabric Size: 50 x 55cm
Stitch Count: 158w x 199h
Design Size: 29 x 35cm

Needle: DMC Cross-Stitch No:26 (Art:1771/3)
Thread: DMC Mouline Stranded Cotton
DMC Floss: B5200, 3822, 963, 3326, 353, 352, 722, 3731, 954, 959, 3812, 907, 906, 905, 3346 and 413
Cross Stitch: 2 strands / **Back Stitch:** 1 strand

Chart on Page 86 - 89

Spread Your Wings and Fly

This charming design feature a timeless and uplifting quote surrounded by pretty foliage. You can never have enough flowers and butterflies, and there are plenty of both to enjoy in this one! It would make a beautiful display on your wall all year round.

materials needed

Fabric: DMC 28ct Linen (DM432SO/B5200)
Colour: White
Fabric Size: 35 x 40cm
Stitch Count: 108w x 118h
Design Size: 19 x 22cm

Needle: DMC Cross-Stitch No:26 (Art:1771/3)
Thread: DMC Mouline Stranded Cotton
DMC Floss: 746, 726, 967, 3341, 341, 165, 166, 580, 772, 988, 986 and 413
Cross Stitch: 2 strands / **Back Stitch:** 1 strand
Chart on Page 90 - 91

Love Grows Here

Show off your green thumb with this set of colourful pots and flowering cactus plants. Just hang this one on your wall anywhere you would like to have a cheery cactus or two!

materials needed

Fabric: DMC 28ct Evenweave (DM542A/Ecru)

Colour: Ecru

Fabric Size: 25 x 30cm

Stitch Count: 56w x 84h

Design Size: 10 x 15cm

Needle: DMC Cross-Stitch No:26 (Art:1771/3)

Thread: DMC Mouline Stranded Cotton

DMC Floss: Blanc, 744, 353, 351, 3716, 962, 907, 906, 3348, 3347, 3346, 168, 169 and 413

Cross Stitch: 2 strands / **Back Stitch:** 1 strand

Chart on Page 82

Welcome to my Garden

This design is perfect for any gardener in your life! It features spring tulips, seed packets, gardening tools and veggies. Try hanging it by the front or back door on the way to the garden, or stitch one or two motifs to use as a greeting card or gift tag.

materials needed

Fabric: DMC 28ct Evenweave (DM542A/Blanc)
Colour: White
Fabric Size: 40 x 40cm
Stitch Count: 120w x 120h
Design Size: 21 x 21cm

Needle: DMC Cross-Stitch No:26 (Art:1771/3)
Thread: DMC Mouline Stranded Cotton
DMC Floss: 712, 3822, 3820, 605, 603, 3801, 3609, 3607, 472, 470, 437, 435, 433, 168, 169 and 413
Cross Stitch: 2 strands / **Back Stitch:** 1 strand
Chart on Page 92 - 93

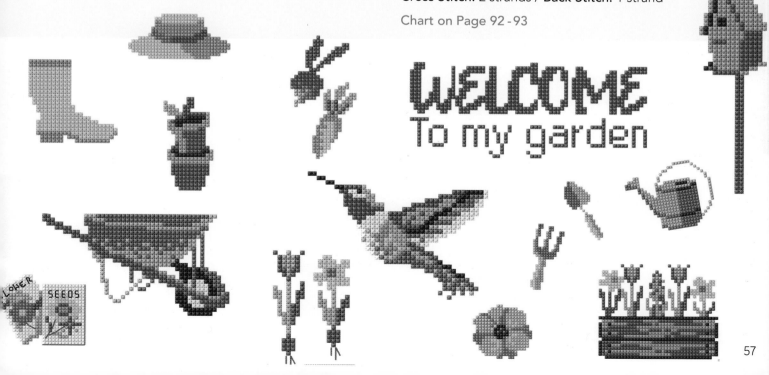

Charts

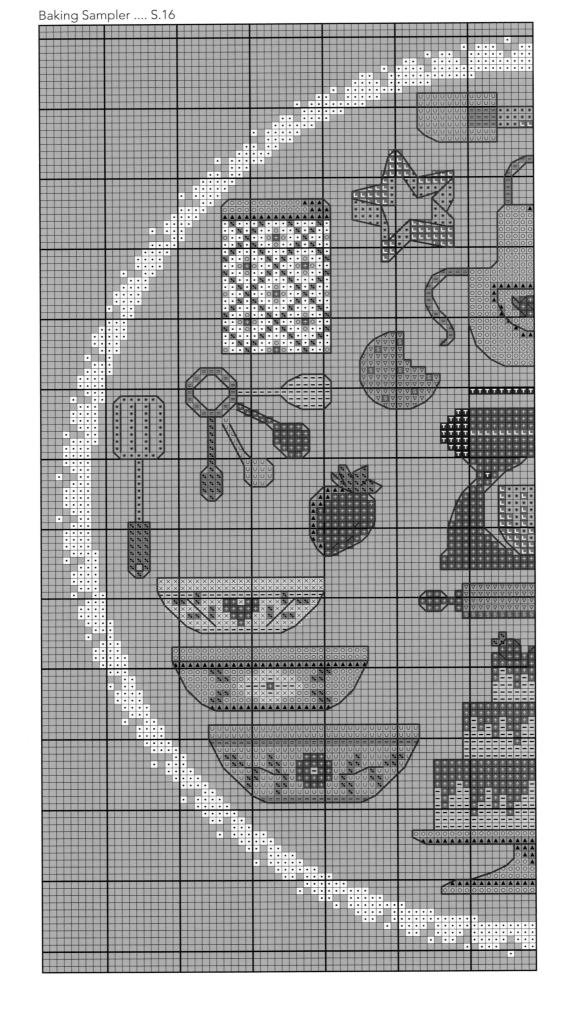

DMC
Mouliné
Stranded Cotton
Art. 117

Symbol	Code
⠂⠂	B5200
×× ××	744
⁻⁻	743
○○ ○○	353
▲▲ ▲▲	352
++ ++	350
U U U U	964
== ==	959
↑↑ ↑↑	3812
%% %%	907
▽▽ ▽▽	437
S S S S	435
** **	168
LL LL	169
TT TT	413
/	413

D·M·C®
Mouliné
Stranded Cotton
Art. 117

::	Ecru	○○	352	UU	3848	SS	904	TT	433	→→	169	/	433
××	677	▲▲	3811	==	3847	**	437	\\	762	II	3799	/	3799
==	353	++	3849	↑↑	906	^^	435	<<	168				

:: 712	== 743	TT 3326	ZZ 309	NN 905	/ 3799		
XX 677	** 436	\\ 899	HH 772	II 168			
-- 745	LL 963	II 335	SS 907	□□ 169			

D·M·C Mouliné Stranded Cotton Art. 117

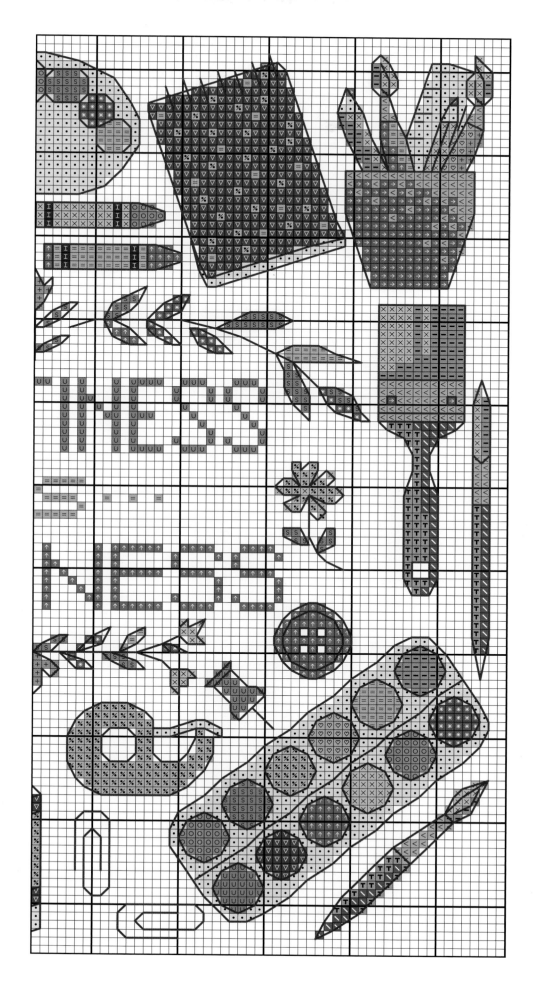

D·M·C

Mouliné
Stranded Cotton
Art. 117

Symbol	Colour
: :	Ecru
× ×	3822
– –	3820
o o	722
♥ ♥	605
+ +	604
U U	3608
= =	964
↑ ↑	958
% %	3761
▽ ▽	3760
S S	166
* *	988
T T	437
\ \	435
< <	168
→ →	169
I I	535
/	535

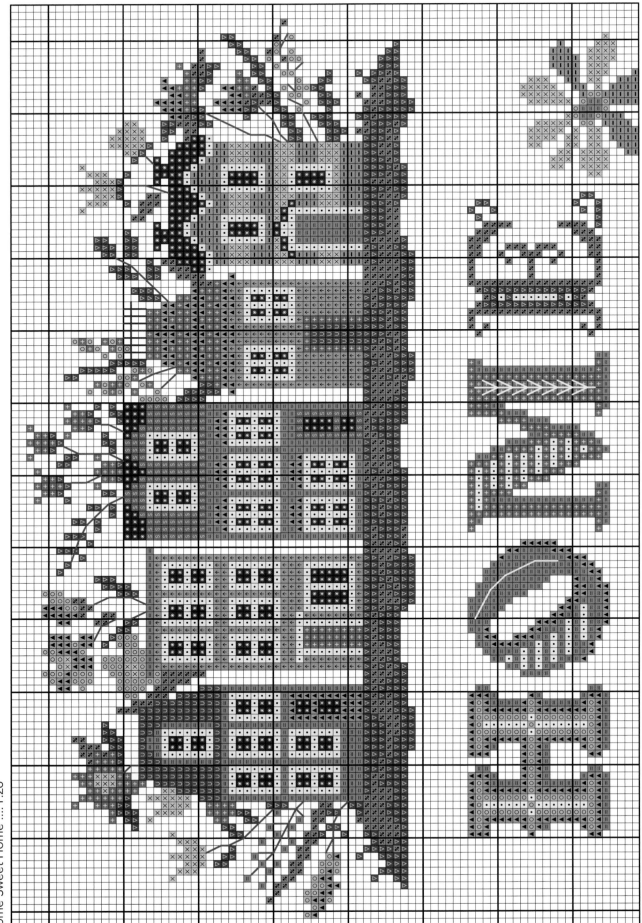

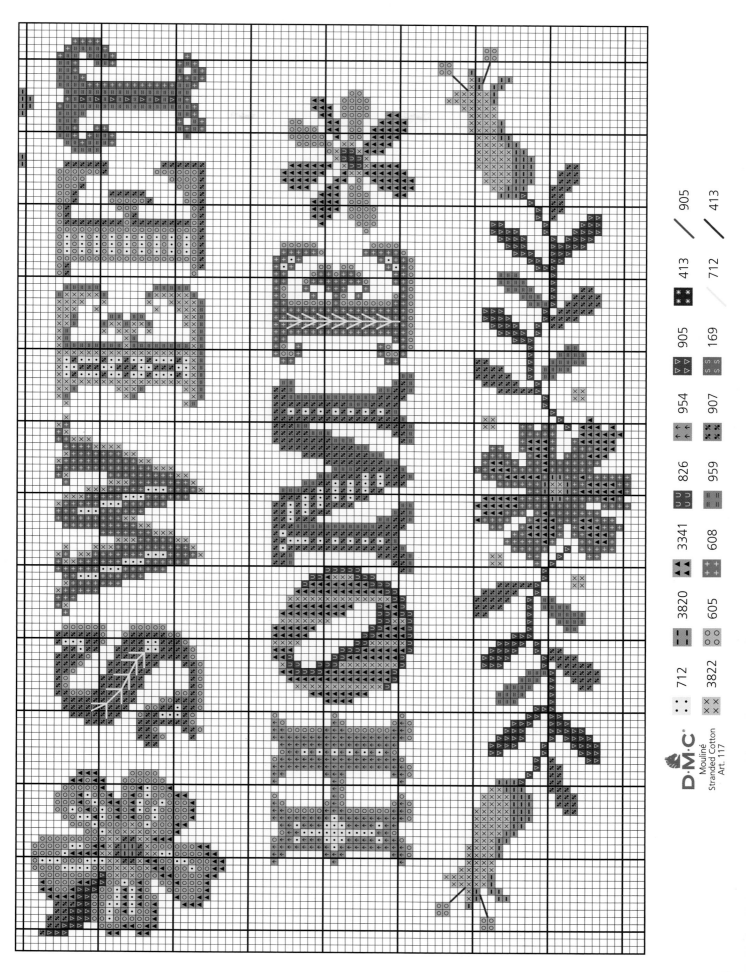

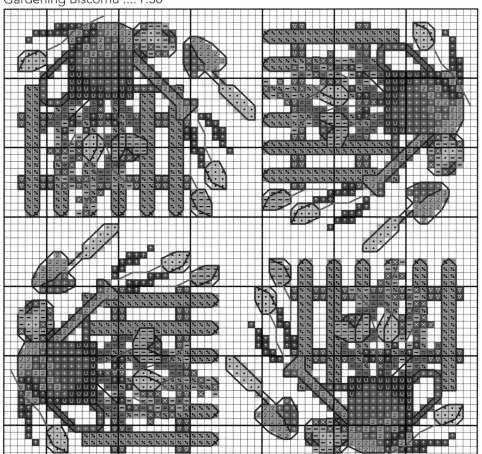

DMC®
Mouliné
Stranded Cotton
Art. 117

: :	3822
- -	3609
× ×	3607
2 2	159
+ +	160
U U	161
= =	989
↑ ↑	987
% %	437
▽ ▽	435
/	413
/	987

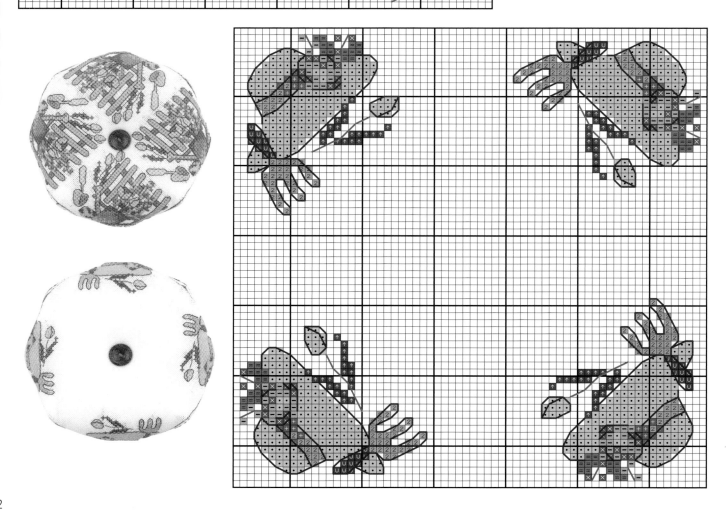

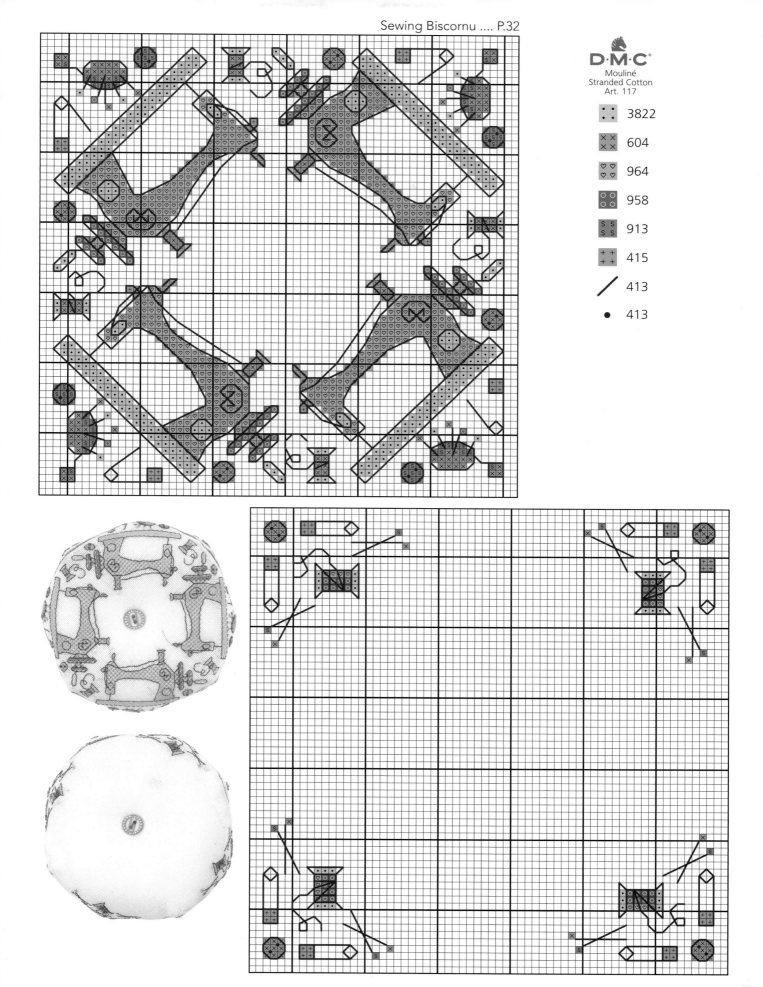

DMC®
Mouliné
Stranded Cotton
Art. 117

: :	3822
× ×	604
♡ ♡	964
○ ○	958
S S	913
+ +	415
/	413
•	413

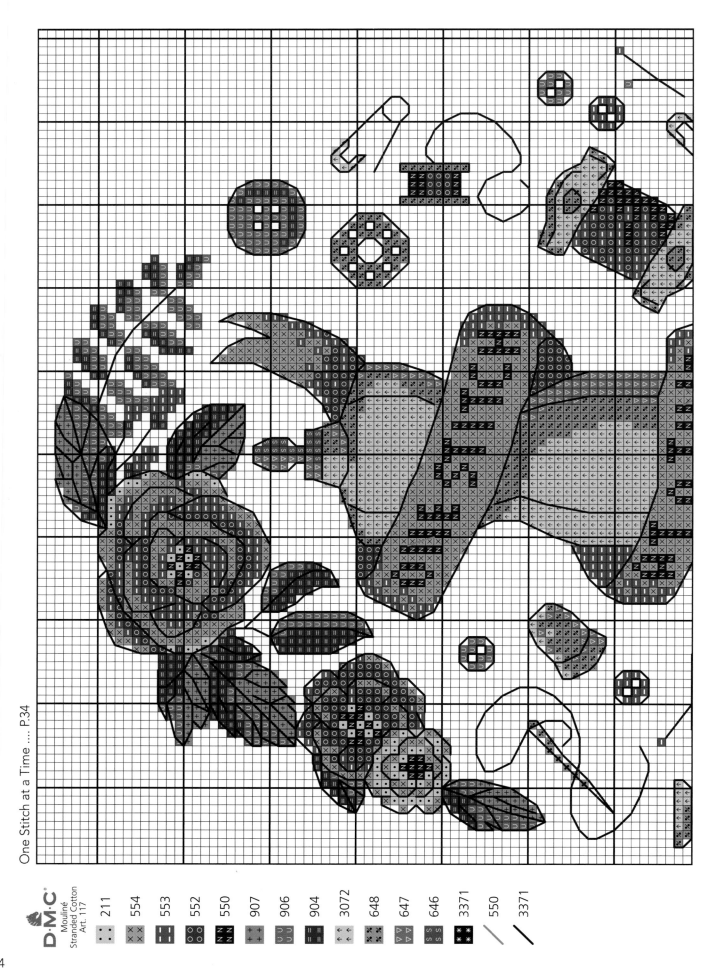

One Stitch at a Time P.34

D·M·C®
Mouliné
Stranded Cotton
Art. 117

	211
	554
	553
	552
	550
	907
	906
	904
	3072
	648
	647
	646
	3371
	550
	3371

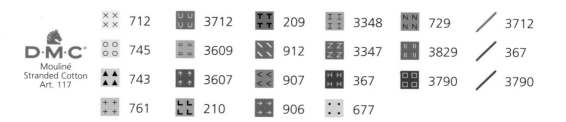

×× 712	UU 3712	TT 209	II 3348	NN 729	╱ 3712
○○ 745	== 3609	◥ 912	ZZ 3347	‖‖ 3829	╱ 367
▲▲ 743	↑↑ 3607	<< 907	HH 367	□□ 3790	╱ 3790
++ 761	LL 210	→→ 906	∴∴ 677		

D·M·C
Mouliné
Stranded Cotton
Art. 117

D·M·C
Mouliné
Stranded Cotton
Art. 117

 Blanc
 3820
 352
 3811
 166
 642
 535

 3822
 353
 921
 3810
 580
 646
/ 535

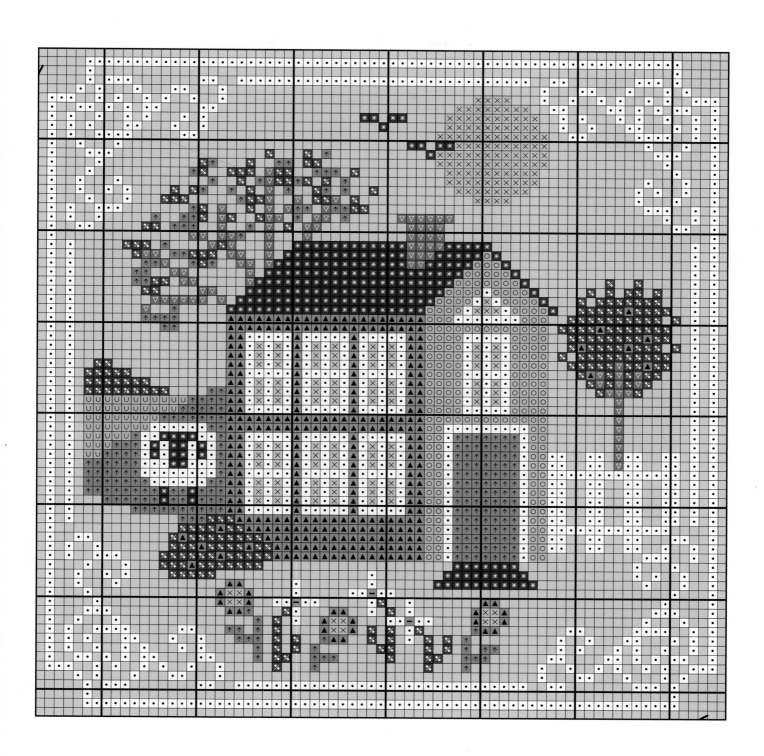

D·M·C
Mouliné
Stranded Cotton
Art. 117

| Blanc |  3820 | ▲▲ 352 | U U
U U 3811 | ↑ ↑
↑ ↑ 166 | ▽ ▽
▽ ▽ 642 | ✳✳ 535 |
| × ×
× × 3822 | ○ ○
○ ○ 353 | + +
+ + 921 | = =
= = 3810 | ✳✳ 580 | s s
s s 646 | / 535 |

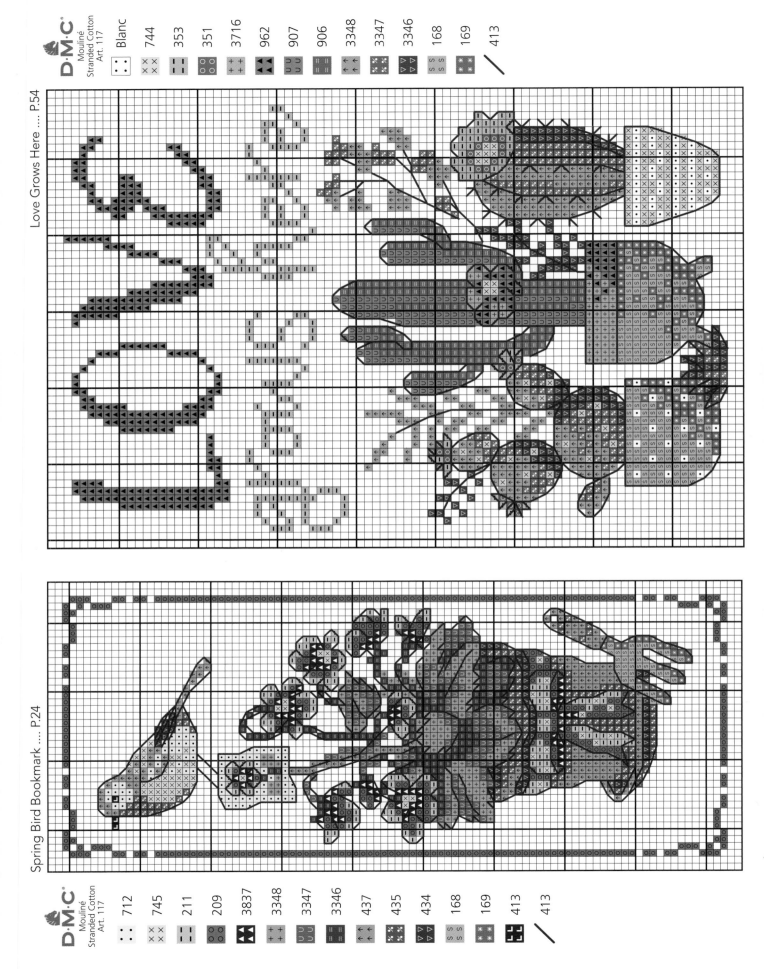

DMC
Mouliné
Stranded Cotton
Art. 117

Blanc	
744	
353	
351	
3716	
962	
907	
906	
3348	
3347	
3346	
168	
169	
413	

Spring Bird Bookmark P.24

DMC
Mouliné
Stranded Cotton
Art. 117

712	
745	
211	
209	
3837	
3348	
3347	
3346	
437	
435	
434	
168	
169	
413	
413	

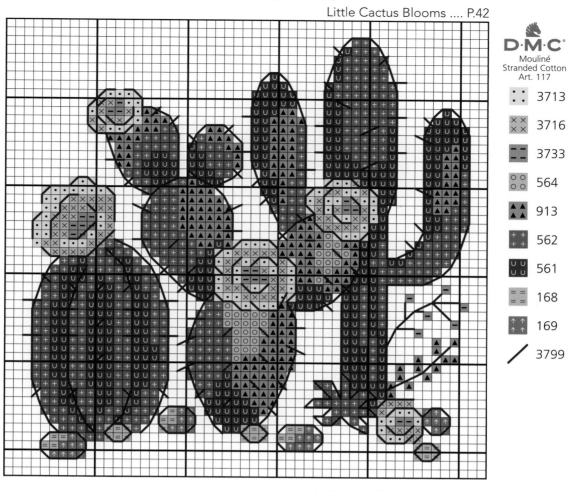

D·M·C
Mouliné
Stranded Cotton
Art. 117

- ⠿ 3713
- ✕✕ 3716
- ━━ 3733
- ○○ 564
- ▲▲ 913
- ++ 562
- UU 561
- ══ 168
- ↑↑ 169
- ╱ 3799

Little House With Wreath P.42

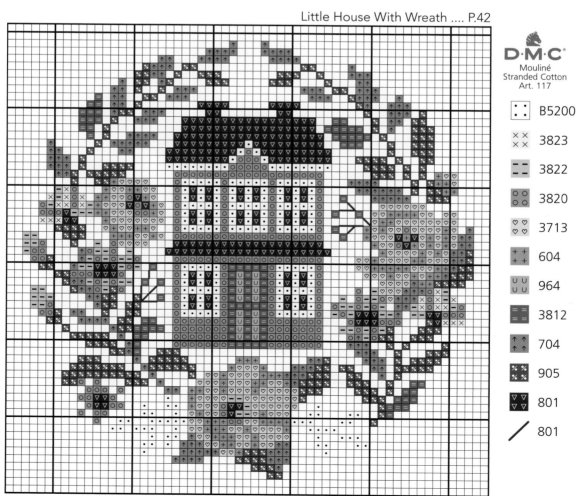

D·M·C
Mouliné
Stranded Cotton
Art. 117

- ⠿ B5200
- ✕✕ 3823
- ══ 3822
- ○○ 3820
- ♡♡ 3713
- ++ 604
- UU 964
- ══ 3812
- ↑↑ 704
- ✕✕ 905
- ▽▽ 801
- ╱ 801

+ + / + +	B5200	o o / o o	353	↑ ↑ / ↑ ↑	747	S S / S S	209	T T / T T	3072	/	3822
× × / × ×	3823	U U / U U	352	% % / % %	519	✱ ✱ / ✱ ✱	955	\ \ / \ \	648	/	954
− − / − −	3822	⊟ ⊟	350	▽ ▽ / ▽ ▽	211	L L / L L	954	< < / < <	646	/	646

DMC
Mouliné
Stranded Cotton
Art. 117

84

D·M·C
Mouliné
Stranded Cotton
Art. 117

712 745 743 353 352 350 164 320 907 470 842 840 169 535 3799 712 350 3799

DMC Mouliné Stranded Cotton Art. 117

∴ B5200	○○ 3326	∪∪ 722	▽▽ 959	∟∟ 906	◄◄ 413 / 413
×× 3822	▲▲ 353	== 3731	ss 3812	тт 905	/ 3822
-- 963	++ 352	%% 954	** 907	◥◥ 3346	/ 905

::	B5200	○○	3326	U U	722	▽	959	L L	906	◄◄	413	/ 413
××	3822	▲▲	353	= =	3731	s s	3812	T T	905	/	3822
--	963	++	352	%%	954	**	907	＼＼	3346	/	905

D·M·C
Mouliné
Stranded Cotton
Art. 117

D·M·C®
Mouliné
Stranded Cotton
Art. 117

Symbol	Code
: :	746
× ×	726
– –	967
o o	3341
♥ ♥	341
+ +	165
* *	166
U U	580
= =	772
↑ ↑	988
⊠ ⊠	986
▽ ▽	413
／	413

D·M·C
Mouliné
Stranded Cotton
Art. 117

Symbol	Color
: :	712
✗ ✗	3822
– –	3820
○ ○	605
Z Z	603
+ +	3801
U U	3609
= =	3607
↑ ↑	472
✕ ✕	470
▽ ▽	437
S S	435
✳ ✳	433
♡ ♡	168
T T	169
◥ ◥	413
╱	470
╱	435
╱	413

THE STITCHES

This section shows how to work the stitches used in the book. When following these instructions, note that stitching is over one block of Aida or two threads of evenweave.

Starting and Finishing Thread

To start off your first length of thread, make a knot at one end and push the needle through to the back of the fabric, about 3cm (1¹/4in) from your starting point, leaving the knot on the right side. Stitch towards the knot, scuring the thread at the back of the fabric as you go. When the thread is secure, cut off the knot.

To finish off a thread or start new threads, simply weave the thread into the back of several stitches.

Cross Stitch

Each coloured square on a chart represents one complete cross stitch. Cross stitch is worked in two easy stages. Start by working one diagonal stitch over one block of Aida or two threads of evenweave, then work a second diagonal stitch over the first stitch, but in the opposite direction to form a cross.

Cross stitches can be worked in rows if you have a large area to cover. Work a row of half cross stitches in one direction and then back in the opposite direction with the diagonal stitches to complete each cross. The upper stitches of all the crosses should lie in the same direction to produce a neat effect.

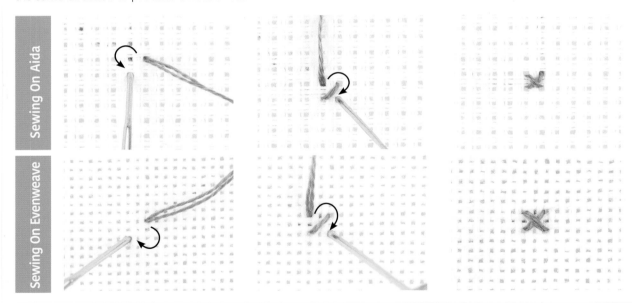

Sewing On Aida

Sewing On Evenweave

Half Cross Stitch

This stitch is also used if you chose to work a design on canvas in tapestry wool (yarn), replacing whole cross stitches with half stitches. A half cross stitch is simply one half of a cross stitch, with the diagonal facing the same way as the upper stitches of each complete cross stitch.

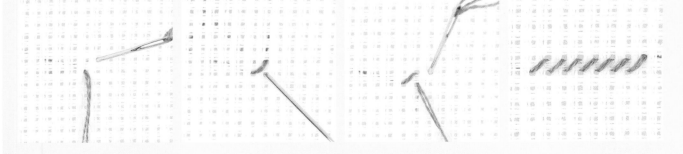

Backstitch

Backstitch is indicated on the charts by a solid coloured line. It is worked around areas of completed cross stitches to add definition, or on top of stitches to add detail.

To work backstitch, pull the needle through the hole in the fabric at 1 and back through at 2. For the next stitch, pull the needle through at 3, then push to the back at 1, and repeat the process to make the next stitch. If working backstitch on an evenweave fabric, wovrk each backstitch over two threads.

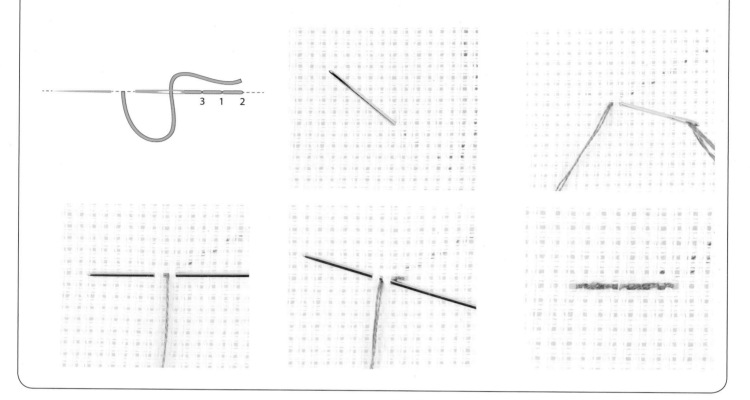

French Knots

These are small knots used for details, indicated on charts by coloured dots.

To work a French knot, bring the needle through to the front of the fabric, just above the point you want the stitch placed. Wind the thread once around the needle and, holding the twisted thread firmly, insert the needle a little away from its starting position. Two tips for working French knots: never rush them and never go back into the same point where your thread came up or your knot will pull through to the back.

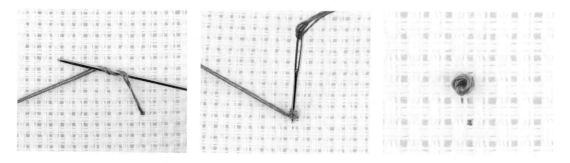

Acknowledgements

None of this would have been possible without my incredible family. Thank you to my husband Scott, for believing in me, and for my kids Mylo and Carson for their encouragement and patience (and opinions!) throughout the process of creating this book.

A very special thanks to my mom, my Grammy, Grandma, great Aunts, and every woman (and man) who practices needlework. It is a proud, valuable tradition that I am honoured to help keep alive.

I would like to extend my sincere thanks to my friends and fellow stitchers, who helped stitch the following models: Alison Gowan, Small things with Great Love; Trina Lucek, Gardening Biscornu, Sewing Biscornu, Welcome to my Garden and Love Grows Here; and Kim Windsor, Spread your Wings and Fly.

You are all awesome!